3 9082 11577 2819

D1398477

SCIENCE IN THE REAL WORLD

How Do Solar Panels Work?

by Richard Hantula

Science and Curriculum Consultant: Debra Voege, M.A.,
Science Curriculum Resource Teacher

CHELSEA CLUBHOUSE

An Imprint of Chelsea House Publishers

Science in the Real World: How Do Solar Panels Work?

Copyright © 2010 by Infobase Publishing

Chelsea Clubhouse
An imprint of Chelsea House Publishers
132 West 31st Street
New York NY 10001

Library of Congress Cataloging-in-Publication Data
Hantula, Richard.
    How do solar panels work? / by Richard Hantula; science and curriculum consultant, Debra Voege.
        p. cm. — (Science in the real world)
    Includes index.
    ISBN 978-1-60413-472-8
    1. Solar energy—Juvenile literature. 2. Solar cells—Juvenile literature. I. Title. II. Series.
TJ810.3.H36 2010
621.31'244—dc22   2009002043

Chelsea Clubhouse books are available at special discounts when purchased in bulk quantities for businesses, associations, institutions, or sales promotions. Please call our Special Sales Department in New York at (212) 967-8800 or (800) 322-8755.

You can find Chelsea Clubhouse on the World Wide Web at http://www.chelseahouse.com

Developed for Chelsea House by RJF Publishing LLC (www.RJFpublishing.com)
Text and cover design by Tammy West/Westgraphix LLC
Illustrations by Spectrum Creative Inc.
Photo research by Edward A. Thomas
Index by Nila Glikin

Photo Credits: 4, 6, 11, 28: iStockphoto; 5: Courtesy NASA/JPL-Caltech; 7, 19, 25: Associated Press; 8: SOHO (ESA and NASA); 10: U.S. Air Force; 12: US Patent and Trademark Office; 13: Courtesy of Smithsonian Institution Libraries, Washington, D.C.; 16: Canyonlands Needles Outpost; 21: Sandia National Laboratory; 26: Alamy.

Printed and bound in the United States of America

Bang RJF 10 9 8 7 6 5 4 3 2 1

This book is printed on acid-free paper.

All links and Web addresses were checked and verified to be correct at the time of publication. Because of the dynamic nature of the Web, some addresses and links may have changed since publication and may no longer be valid.

Table of Contents

Words that are defined in the Glossary are in **bold** type
the first time they appear in the text.

Endless Energy

Energy comes in different forms. Light is a form of energy. So is heat. So is electricity.

Often, one form of energy can be turned into another. This fact is very important because it explains how we get electricity, which we use in so many ways. Electricity is used to light streets and buildings, to run computers and TVs, and to run many other machines and appliances at home, at school, and at work.

One way to get electricity is to burn a fuel like oil or coal. This makes heat. The heat then makes water boil and turn into steam. The steam runs a machine called a **turbine** that produces electricity. Often, this electricity then goes into a public power system that sends it out, through wires, to homes, schools, and businesses over a wide area.

This method for making electricity is popular. But it has some problems. Our planet has only a limited supply of oil and coal. They are not **renewable** fuels. Once they are

Electricity is a key form of energy. It powers all the lights visible in this view of Seattle, Washington.

used, they are gone forever. Also, they give off gases when they are burned. These gases may make the air dirty, or polluted, and some of them may change Earth's climate.

Free and Clean Energy

Another way to make electricity uses sunlight. Sunshine is free and never gets used up. Also, there is a lot of it. The sunlight that hits the Earth in an hour has more energy than the people of the world use in a year.

A little device called a **solar cell** can make electricity right from sunlight ("solar" means having to do with the Sun). A solar cell doesn't give off any gases. It doesn't even make any noise. A **solar panel** is a group of solar cells that work together.

The use of solar cells is growing fast in the United States and many other countries.

Solar panels supply the electricity used by this "rover" as it explores the planet Mars.

DID YOU KNOW ?

Power in Remote Places

Solar panels are a handy way of getting electricity in very remote places where there is no public power system. They power runway lights at airstrips in Antarctica. They are used in spacecraft and in "rovers" on the planet Mars.

Solar Cells Galore

Solar cells and solar panels have lots of uses. They are in everyda things like calculators, watches, and flashlights. There are solar-powered toys, radios, and MP3 players. There are solar-powered cell phones and pagers. Using **solar power** with devices like these means you never have to worry about batteries.

Solar panels are sometimes used to make the electricity to light up road signs and bus stops. They may make the electricity that makes roadside emergency phones or parking meters work. Even some ATMs (machines that let you get money from or pu money into your bank account) have solar panels.

Power for Buildings

The ceiling lights and all kinds of

Houses with solar panels often have them on the roof.

machines and appliances used at home, school, and work get their electricity from the wires running through the building. Usually, this electricity comes to the building from the

The solar-powered Zephyr can stay in the air for days at a time.

public power system, or **grid**. But solar panels can also be used along with power from the grid. People sometimes put solar panels on their homes. Large buildings may have them as well. They make it possible to use less of the grid's costly electricity. In addition, they are a backup in case of a power failure, or blackout.

In some areas the grid itself gets some power from solar panels.

DID YOU KNOW ?

Solar Planes

Solar panels have even been used on airplanes—but only on a few. The problem is they are hard to use with planes. They need to cover a big area in order to make enough electricity. When it gets dark, they don't work. The first solar-powered plane to fly a long distance was the Solar Challenger. It crossed the English Channel in Europe in 1981. Its wings had more than 16,000 solar cells. In 2008 the Zephyr-6 spent more than three days in the air. It was a plane without any pilot. It carried batteries that stored electricity from its panels for use at night.

Energy from Sunshine

The Sun constantly gives off energy. The energy is carried through space as **electromagnetic radiation**. There are several types of electromagnetic radiation. Light is one type. Radio waves are another.

Electromagnetic radiation travels like waves in water. Like water waves, it is a series of ups and downs. One way various types of electromagnetic waves differ is in their **wavelength**. This is the distance between two ups (or two downs) in a row. The wavelengths of radio waves are longer than those of light. Among types of light, red has a longer wavelength than blue.

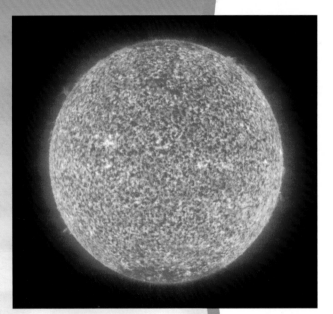

The Sun blazes with energy.

How Solar Cells Use Light

Only part of the energy sent toward Earth by the Sun actually makes it to Earth's surface. Some solar energy gets bounced back into space. Some gets absorbed by the air. Most of the

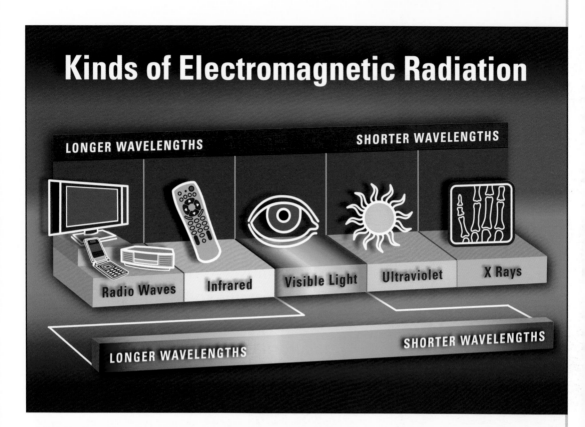

Kinds of Electromagnetic Radiation

LONGER WAVELENGTHS   SHORTER WAVELENGTHS

Radio Waves   Infrared   Visible Light   Ultraviolet   X Rays

LONGER WAVELENGTHS   SHORTER WAVELENGTHS

solar energy that does make it to Earth's surface is in the form of visible light. Solar cells can use the energy of this light to make electricity. But they don't work equally well with all forms of light. Different types of solar cells use different wavelengths. This means a cell can use only some of the solar energy that it receives.

Different kinds of electro-magnetic radiation have different wavelengths. Solar cells use certain wavelengths of visible light to make electricity.

DID YOU KNOW ?

Photovoltaic

Another name for solar cells is photovoltaic cells. This name is fitting, because photo means "light" and voltaic refers to electricity.

Under-standing Electricity

People often think of electricity as something that flows. In fact, that is pretty much right. Electricity is a stream of tiny particles called electrons. The stream is called an electric current.

There are two kinds of current. One is **DC**. This is direct current. It always flows in the same direction. Batteries and solar cells make DC. The other kind of current is **AC**. This is alternating current. It reverses direction many times a second. The grid has AC. Most home electrical devices use AC.

Solar panels at Nellis Air Force Base in Nevada. Nellis's photovoltaic solar power plant is the biggest in the United States.

Measuring Electricity

Electric power is the rate at which electric energy is used. It is measured in **watts**. A 100-watt light bulb is more powerful than a 60-watt bulb. It uses more electricity. (When people talk about large numbers of watts, they use larger units: a kilowatt is 1,000 watts; a megawatt is 1 million watts.)

Another important unit is the watt-hour. It measures the electric energy produced or used during a period of time. It equals 1 watt of power over a period of one hour. A similar but larger unit is the **kilowatt-hour**. This is 1,000 watts over an hour. A 100-watt light bulb that stays on for 10 hours uses 1,000 watt-hours of electric energy. This amount is the same as 1 kilowatt-hour.

This typical electricity meter measures how many kilowatt-hours are being used.

DID YOU KNOW ?

Finding Electrons

An electric current is not the only place one can find electrons. They are also in the small particles called atoms that make up everything we see around us. Each atom has a center, called the nucleus. This contains at least one particle called a proton. In most types of atoms the nucleus has several protons and other particles called neutrons. One or more electrons usually circle around the nucleus.

Looking Back

Edmond Becquerel of France first noticed that light can cause materials to make electricity. This was in 1839. Other scientists later studied the ties between light, matter, and electricity. One of them was Albert Einstein. In 1905 he explained how atoms take in electromagnetic radiation (such as light) and then give off electrons. This process is called the photoelectric effect. Einstein won the Nobel Prize in 1921 for his work on it.

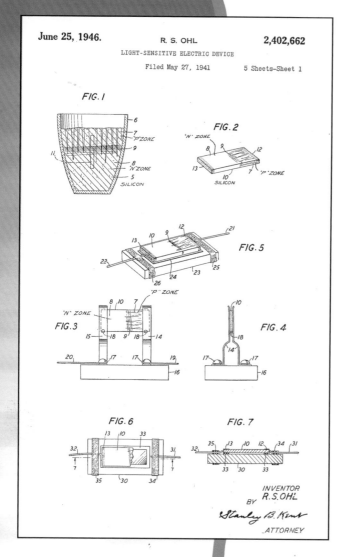

The first page of Russell Ohl's 1941 application for a patent on his solar cell.

The First Solar Cells

Russell Ohl was the first person to come up with a solar cell like the ones used today. He worked at Bell Laboratories in New Jersey. His cell was made of silicon (silicon is found in sand and in many types of rock). He called the cell a "light-sensitive electric device." He filed for a **patent** on it in 1941. Five years later, he got the patent. In 1954, Bell Labs made the first practical solar cell. It was the first one to make enough electricity to run ordinary electrical devices.

Still, early cells didn't make much electricity. Also, they were very costly. Their first important use was in space satellites, starting in 1958. As cells became cheaper, they were used in other ways. The first power station able to make 1 megawatt of electricity with solar panels opened in Hesperia, California, in 1982.

Edmond Becquerel

Edmond Becquerel (above) lived for more than 70 years, from 1820 to 1891. He worked in a lot of research areas. They included light, electricity, and magnetism. His discovery of electricity from light came in 1839, when he was only 19 years old. Edmond's son Henri became even more famous than his father. In 1896, Henri discovered radioactivity.

Inside a Solar Cell

Solar cells come in various sizes. Some are tinier than a stamp. Some are 5 inches (12 centimeters) across.

The cells are made of a type of material known as a **semiconductor**. Often, they are made of silicon. Semiconductors can conduct, or carry, electricity. They don't do this as well as metals, however. That is why they are called "semi." Because they only "semi" conduct electricity, they can be used to control electric current. On their top and bottom they typically have metal contacts through which current can flow.

A typical simple cell has two layers of silicon. One is known as n-type. The other is p-type. The layers are different from each other.

How Solar Cells Make Electricity

The process of making electricity begins when the silicon atoms absorb some light. The light's energy knocks some electrons out of the atoms. The electrons flow between the two layers. The flow makes an

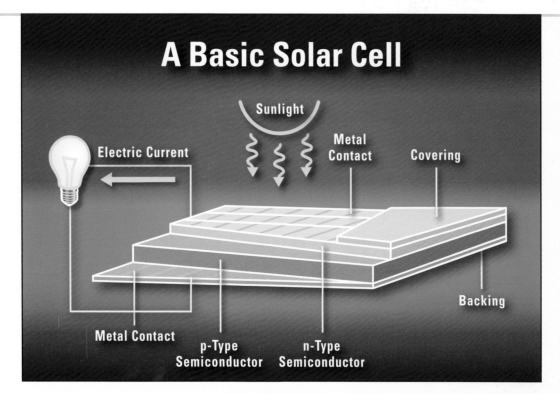

A Basic Solar Cell

Sunlight

Electric Current

Metal Contact

Covering

Backing

Metal Contact

p-Type Semiconductor

n-Type Semiconductor

electric current. The current can leave the cell through the metal contacts and be used.

When light hits a solar cell, much of its energy is wasted. Some light bounces off or passes through the cell. Some is turned into heat. Only light with the right wavelengths, or colors, is absorbed and then turned into electricity.

A typical simple solar cell uses some sunlight to make electricity that flows between the two semiconductor layers. This electric current leaves the cell through the metal contacts and can be used.

DID YOU KNOW ?

A Different Kind of Solar Cell

Some solar cells are made from very, very thin layers of material. The layers are thinner than four ten-thousandths of an inch (10 micrometers, or a thousandth of a centimeter). Some of these "thin-film" cells have, like ordinary solar cells, a rigid backing. Others have a flexible backing. Thin-film cells are good for making lightweight or flexible panels. They also are good for covering a large area, such as the walls of a building.

Cells + Cells + Cells

A single simple solar cell makes only a little electricity. For most purposes more is needed. For this reason, cells are often linked together in groups known as **solar modules**. A solar module has a frame that holds the cells. Some modules are several feet long and wide. They usually can produce up to a few hundred watts of electricity. If more power is needed, modules can be joined together to form a large **solar array**.

Modules are sometimes called solar panels. Arrays are also sometimes called solar panels. Whatever you call a group of solar cells, the fact remains: the more cells you link together, the more electricity you make.

With enough modules, huge amounts of power are possible. A good example is a new power plant being built at Moura in Portugal. The first phase of the project has 262,080 solar modules, each with 48 cells. They will produce up to 46 megawatts of electricity.

This solar array supplies power to a general store and campground in Utah.

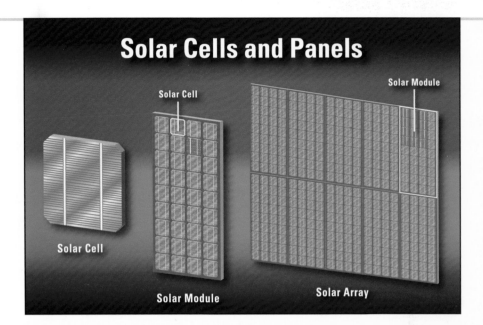

Solar Cells and Panels

Solar Module

Solar Cell

Solar Cell

Solar Module

Solar Array

More Power

Many experts think even bigger power plants using solar panels will be built in the coming years. Someday there may be solar plants able to make as much as 500 megawatts of power. That is about what a typical coal power plant produces today.

Solar panels work best when they directly face the Sun. For this reason, the panels are often put on "trackers." The trackers turn the panels so that they follow the Sun as it moves across the sky.

To make more electricity, solar cells can be linked together in a solar module, and many modules can be joined together in a solar array.

DID YOU KNOW ?

Concentrated Sunshine

Solar cells work better with bright light. In order to let modules receive as much light as possible, sometimes **concentrators** are used. These are devices that collect sunlight over a large area. They use mirrors or lenses to focus the light on the solar modules. Since concentrators have to be pointed right at the Sun, they are mounted on trackers.

Panels on Homes and Other Buildings

Solar panels for buildings are no different from other panels. They must be able to receive enough sunlight to be useful.

Often, they are put on a roof that faces the Sun and is not shaded. Sometimes they are simply built on the ground.

Solar panels come in various colors and designs. They may be put on a wall or roof and blend right in, so you don't even notice them. Roof shingles and tiles can be made using thin-film panels.

Homes with solar panels usually have an inverter that changes DC electricity to AC. The home shown below can also get electricity from the power grid, and it can send any extra electricity it makes to the grid.

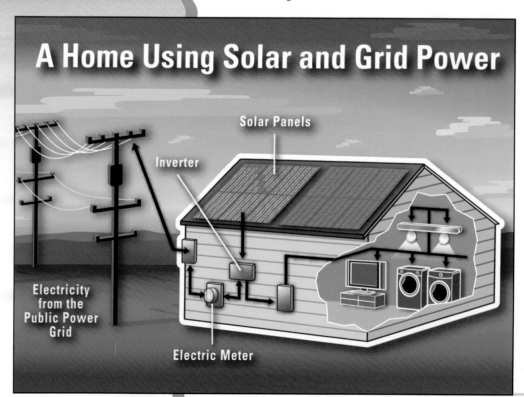

A Home Using Solar and Grid Power

Solar Panels

Inverter

Electricity from the Public Power Grid

Electric Meter

Usually solar panels and a few wires cannot by themselves supply electricity to a building. More equipment is needed. Solar cells make DC electricity. This is fine for some electronic devices. But home appliances and lights usually run on AC. Houses are generally wired for AC. To change the DC to AC, a device called an inverter is needed.

Storing Electricity

Also, if the building is not connected to the public power grid, there has to be some way of storing electricity for use when it is too dark for the solar panels to work. Usually, batteries are used to store the electricity. Batteries can be helpful even in buildings that are connected to the grid. They can serve as a backup if the grid suffers a power loss.

Parts of the south and east faces of the Condé Nast Building in New York City include thin-film solar panels.

DID YOU KNOW ?

Net Metering

Power from the grid costs money. If some of a home's power comes from solar panels, the home can use less grid power. But there's another way solar panels can cut electric bills. A U.S. law passed in 2005 required electric companies to offer "net metering." This is a special program for people who are customers of electric companies and also have solar panels. With net metering, if customers have extra solar power—power they produce but don't use—this power is bought by the electric company.

Good Things About Solar Panels

Solar panels have a lot of strong points. The silicon used in most of them is a very common material. Sand is made up mostly of silicon. Solar panels are reliable. The "fuel" they use—sunshine—is free. It is a renewable resource that will last nearly forever. Scientists expect the Sun to keep shining for billions of years. Also, solar panels can make electricity right at the place where it is used. This removes the need for wires or cables to carry electricity from a distant power plant.

When they are used, solar panels have almost no effect on the environment. They are quiet. They don't release dirty or harmful gases into the air. They don't cause water pollution. They don't create hazardous waste.

Cleaner Power Plants

Power plants using solar panels have several advantages. They can usually be built more quickly than oil, coal, or nuclear power plants. If more power is needed, they are easier to expand than other types of power

"Troughs" for collecting solar energy at a huge solar thermal power plant at Kramer Junction, California.

plants. Oil and coal power plants use huge amounts of fuel. This fuel can be expensive, and burning it causes pollution. The process of carrying the fuel to power plants can also cause environmental problems. For solar panel power plants, these problems do not exist.

DID YOU KNOW ?

Another Kind of Solar Power

Solar panels are not the only way to make electricity from sunshine. Another method—called solar thermal power—is also popular. In fact, it is used in the largest solar power plants. Solar thermal power plants collect sunlight with the help of concentrators. Often, the light heats a liquid to a high temperature, and this hot liquid then turns water into steam. Or the light may directly heat water and turn it into steam. Either way, the steam is then used to drive a turbine that makes electricity. Small thermal systems are sometimes used in buildings to provide heating or make hot water.

Concerns About Solar Panels

A long with strong points, solar panels have some weak points. For one thing, they work best when the Sun shines brightly. When the sky is cloudy, they make less electricity. In the United States, southern states tend to get more sunshine than, say, cloudy Washington in the Northwest. In order to make the same amount of electricity, a house in Washington will probably need more panels than a house in Arizona.

One problem is the same everywhere. When it's dark, solar panels don't work at all. If a solar-powered home isn't linked to the grid, it needs

This map shows, for the month of June, which parts of the 48 contiguous U.S. states typically get more sunshine and which get less.

Where the Sun Shines

Most Sunshine

Least Sunshine

to have batteries or some other way to store electricity for use at night.

The Price of Solar Panels

While sunshine is free, solar panels are not. Getting a solar system for a building costs money. In many cases today, the total cost may turn out to be so high that it's cheaper to get power from the grid. This may change in the future, though, as the cost of electricity made by power plants using oil goes up. Also, as more solar panels are used, the price of the panels may come down.

Solar power plants that are able to make large amounts of electricity need large amounts of land—and also lots of solar panels that are costly today.

DID YOU KNOW ?

Environmental Questions

Solar panels use a renewable resource. Compared to other ways of making electricity, they are very clean. But they are not perfect. It takes energy to get silicon ready for use in a solar cell. It takes more energy to make the cells and panels. This energy usually comes from burning nonrenewable fuels like coal or oil. Burning them puts gases that cause pollution into the air.

Factories that make solar cells produce very little hazardous waste. But still there is some.

Solar panels that are used for many years wear out. Experts are working on finding ways to recycle them.

Giving Solar Power a Boost

Most electricity used in the United States comes from the public power grid. Sometimes the demand for power is almost more than the grid can handle. People can help out by making some of their own electricity. This eases the load on the grid. But that's not all it can do. Using a renewable "fuel" like sunlight to make electricity saves on nonrenewable fuels, such as oil or coal. It also avoids the pollution that comes from burning oil or coal.

Of course, another good way to reduce use of nonrenewable fuels is to just use less electricity. People can cut down on how much electricity they use simply by doing things like switching off the lights when they leave a room.

Promoting Solar Power

There are government programs in the United States to promote solar power. Some users pay less in taxes. In 2006, the Energy Department began a "Solar America Initiative." This program helps scientists who are researching ways to cut the cost of solar technology. An Energy Department program called Building America promotes the use of renewable energy, such as solar power. Its research projects have built more than 40,000 homes. Its goal is a "zero-energy" home. Such a house would make as much energy as it used.

Contests help spur interest in solar power. Every two or three years since 2002, the Energy Department has sponsored a "Solar Decathlon." It's an event for college students. Teams compete to design, build, and operate the best solar-powered house.

A solar-powered car from the University of Michigan won the 2008 North American Solar Challenge.

DID YOU KNOW ?

Solar Cars

In December 2008 an experimental solar-powered car called the Solar-taxi completed an around-the-world trip. It was driven more than 30,000 miles (50,000 kilometers) using an electric motor powered by solar cells. In the World Solar Challenge, held every two years, solar-powered cars race across Australia. The United States and Canada have their own race, the North American Solar Challenge. It also is held every other year. The U.S. Energy Department sponsors a contest for sixth, seventh, and eighth graders. It is called the National Junior Solar Sprint. Student teams build and race model solar-powered cars.

Solar Cells Get Better and Better

When experts compare solar cells, one thing they look at is how costly a cell is. If it costs too much, nobody will buy it. One problem with the first solar cells was that they usually cost more than other power sources. That is why the first important use of solar cells was in space satellites. There were no cheaper ways to make electricity in space in the 1950s.

Another thing experts look at is a cell's "efficiency." This tells how good a cell is at using sunlight. A high-efficiency cell turns more of the sunlight's energy into electric energy than a low-efficiency cell.

The EcoTech Centre in Norfolk, England, gets power from the wind as well as solar panels.

Ever since solar cells were invented, scientists have worked to make them cheaper and more efficient. There has been a lot of progress. The first solar cells had an efficiency of less than 4 percent. Today cells cost a lot less, and many have an efficiency of 15 percent or more. Some experimental cells do even better.

Making Better Solar Cells

Scientists continue to hunt for ways to make better cells. They are trying new materials, such as plastics. They are also looking for ways solar cells and panels can be more useful. For instance, they have come up with a "photocapacitor." This is a solar device that both makes electricity and stores it for later use. Experimental models were not good for practical use. But if the device can be improved, it might someday eliminate the need to have batteries to store solar electricity, at least in some cases.

DID YOU KNOW ?

Sun Plus Wind

When the Sun doesn't shine, solar panels can't make electricity. But there is a renewable energy source that can: the wind. Some people have electric power systems that combine solar panels with a wind turbine. Such a system is called a hybrid. Of course, the wind doesn't always blow at night. So if the system has no link with the grid, it will still need batteries for electricity on windless nights.

More Solar Products

People keep coming up with new ideas for solar energy. They dream up new designs for solar cells. They think of new materials for cells. The new kinds of solar cells that result make possible new ways of using solar energy. Lots of ideas for solar products have been talked about in recent years. Some of them have begun to appear on the market. Others are still experimental.

Scientists are working on ways to make electricity using sunlight that passes through windows.

Ideas for the Future

Thin-film solar cells can be put into cloth. The larger the area of the solar cells, the more current they can make. If they were used in curtains, thin-film solar cells could provide a very useful amount of electricity.

Many people think devices called hydrogen **fuel cells** might someday be very good sources of power for many purposes. They use hydrogen to make electricity. Hydrogen is very common. It is in water, for instance. Getting the hydrogen out of water, however, takes energy. If solar panels get cheap enough and efficient enough, they might become a practical way of providing this energy.

Ways of getting lots of sunlight to solar cells are being studied. One proposed concentrator could be used on windows. It involves putting special dyes into glass or plastic. Solar cells are put at the edges of the sheet of glass or plastic. The dyes let some light through the window. They also capture some light energy, which flows to the cells.

DID YOU KNOW ?

Power from Space

In space there are no clouds. Solar panels there can get lots of sunshine. Scientists have proposed using huge solar arrays on satellites to make power. The power would then be beamed down to Earth for use. A big question is whether long-distance beams are practical. An experiment in 2008 managed to send a small amount of energy about 90 miles (150 kilometers). The experiment, which took place in Hawaii, used radio waves to carry the energy.

Glossary

AC—"Alternating current": a type of electric current that reverses its direction many times a second.

concentrator—A way of collecting lots of sunlight over a large area and sending it to a **solar panel**, which has a smaller area. Concentrators often use lenses or mirrors.

DC—"Direct current": a type of electric current that always flows in the same direction.

electromagnetic radiation—Energy that moves through space as waves. Light is one type. Radio waves are another.

fuel cell—A device that uses a reaction between two substances to make electricity.

grid—The general electric power system.

kilowatt-hour—A common unit of measurement used with electricity. It involves 1,000 **watts** of power acting for a period of one hour.

patent—For an invention, a document giving its holder the right to make and sell the invention. The patent also prevents others from making and selling the invention without the holder's permission.

renewable—A resource, such as a source of energy, that never gets used up. Energy sources such as sunlight and wind are renewable. Energy sources such as coal, gas, and oil are "nonrenewable."

semiconductor—A substance that conducts electricity, but not as well as a metal.

solar array—A group of **solar modules** that are linked together.

solar cell— A little device that makes electricity from sunlight.

solar module—A group of **solar cells** that are linked together.

solar panel—Another name for a **solar module** or **solar array**.

solar power—Energy from the Sun that is put to practical use, such as the production of electricity.

turbine—A machine with a turning action that can be used to make electricity.

watt—A common unit of measurement for the rate at which electric energy is used.

wavelength—The distance between two successive upbeats (or downbeats) of a wave. Red light has a longer wavelength than blue.

To Learn More

Read these books:

Povey, Karen D. *Energy Alternatives*. Detroit: Lucent, 2007.

Thomas, Isabel. *The Pros and Cons of Solar Power*. New York: Rosen, 2007.

Walker, Niki. *Harnessing Power from the Sun*. New York: Crabtree, 2006.

Look up these Web sites:

California Energy Commission, Energy Quest Room
http://www.energyquest.ca.gov

**Department of Energy, Office of Energy Efficiency
and Renewable Energy**
http://www.eere.energy.gov/kids/renergy.html

Energy Information Administration, Kid's Page
http://www.eia.doe.gov/kids

How Stuff Works
http://www.howstuffworks.com/solar-cell.htm

**National Renewable Energy Laboratory,
Junior Solar Sprint/Hydrogen Fuel Cell Car Competitions**
http://www.nrel.gov/education/jss_hfc.html

Key Internet search terms:

electricity, solar cells, solar panels, solar power

Index

About the Author

Richard Hantula has written, edited, and translated books and articles on science and technology for more than three decades. He was the senior U.S. editor for the *Macmillan Encyclopedia of Science*.